For Suhad and Haider, the two people that gave
me everything to be who I am today.

To order additional copies of this book, contact:
Xlibris
844-714-8691
www.Xlibris.com
Orders@Xlibris.com

ISBN: Softcover   978-1-6641-5764-4
         EBook   978-1-6641-5729-3

Print information available on the last page

Rev. date: 02/19/2021

Table of Contents

Thoughts

My thoughts carried me
And they carried you
Through the thickest of storms
I'm one of the very few

My thoughts married you
And cared through your pain
My thoughts paid your dues
In the snow, mud and rain

My thoughts raised a family
And laughed and screamed with you
Your smile kept my sanity
My thoughts died with you.

Flutter

Pure beauty
Walking like one of us
Fluttering away
With no one she can trust

Her smile
Her beautiful eyes
Speak for miles
A pure soul that was once told lies

And there she goes
Fluttering away
And no one knows
If she'll come back to stay.

Rose

I'm screaming but my eyes won't open
I'm seeing but my mouth is closed
I can't hear anything anymore
So I went away to look for my rose

I passed a dandelion
I placed it in my ear
This is my rose for now
Yet it made me shed a tear

I placed it where I found it
I kept searching in my highs and lows
Then I found a mustard seed
And I forgot about my rose

Then the mustard seed hurt me
So I set it down to grow on its own
Maybe it's not me who should look for the rose
Maybe the rose is supposed to find me

So I gave it up
And lived alone
Sitting in the sun
On a bench of stone

Then out of the cracks of the bench
Was a green growing glow
I watched it
Yet I let it grow on its own

It's been some time now
And what do you know
The rose came
But it waited for me to grow.

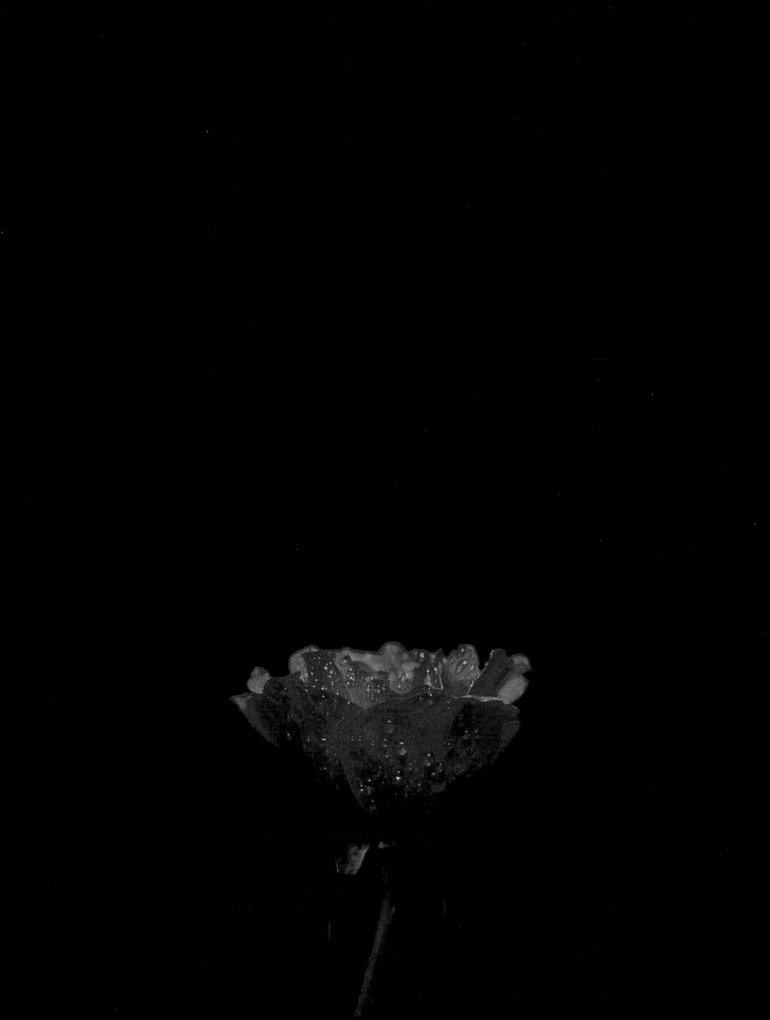

Chase

It's been four long years
Running and dodging at my pace
My mind is not clear
Now every demon has a face

Laughter and smiles by day
Showing what I desire to be seen
It comes back in the night to say
I control your life and your dreams

So I sit and ponder
Do I continue the chase?
I run and wonder
Am I meant to lose this race?

Minute peaks
Deep troughs
My spirit is weak
My armor has become soft

So let me stop and end the chase
It's time I ceased running
Let me look at the vile disgrace
I see in myself while thinking

Help me let go of the Hope
Of a sliver of a better day
Untie the knots and cut the ropes
I don't believe I'm meant to stay

So this is farewell
From the Man in His Mind
Broken by the fallen angels of Hell
So live, and Love you may find.

Beauty

Her presence reminds me
Of the fruits of living here
Her smile confides in me
And washes away my fear

An uncontrollable feeling
Of vines growing up from death's door
Squeezing-strangling-swallowing
Everything in its path until it reaches the core

When it gets there
It softens and cradles
A moment that is only rare
To men who live among fables

Here she comes!
Stay quiet and see
How her mere presence
Can delude a man like me.

Starlit Delusion

In the form of a comforting blanket
Charges in the worst of them all
Like cavalry horses blinded
Ready to cut their chord before their master falls

They scream in whispers through my ears
They are the midnight illusions
Yet once they feel the heat of a single tear
They become Starlit Delusions

Crashing like the rising tide
The blanketed horses charge
They stomp and trample my soul and I
For every gallop has become large

Without my knowledge
I've let them grow
I've opened up my drawbridge
The hordes charge like the water flows

My eyes see defeat
My mind feels pain
Yet there is one sliver of hope
That makes me feel no shame

It is my Starlit Delusion
Infested with confusion
Riddled with illusion
Marking one of many conclusions.

My Time

It has taken me pain and growth to find
The one set to swim through crashing waves
He is the Man in His Mind
His spirit is true yet his mind does not behave

His image dies without correlation
Himself he truly sees
A king without a coronation
A drop in the ocean that flees

He thought they believed
Believed in his innermost self
Self-taught in the ways of the deceived
Deceived by his world and himself.

Have You

Have you ever felt fear
To lay in a quiet moment of sleep
Have you felt your end drawing near
Plummeting down, dark and deep

Have you seen what I've seen?
The beauty of pure happiness and Love
Have you seen what I've seen?
Attached to your demons like a glove

Have you heard what I've heard?
Morning trains and birds rejoicing
Have you heard what I've heard?
Screams in pain that are blood-curdling

Have you touched what I've touched?
A beautiful person's face
Have you touched what I've touched?
The thoughts of every color, creed and race

Have you felt what I've felt?
The happiness of accomplishment
Have you felt what I've felt?
A loved one's soul as you lament

Do you think you know?
I am determined to say not
Through every ebb and flow
Walking in my footsteps for those who cannot.

Escape of Promise

They left their home for me
All of their belongings
They left the family
So I could see a world that was harmless

They lived through occupation
A people in need of saving
The perils of war, death and starvation
Needing love that all of them are craving

In hopes of promise
We escaped
The hot land of the heartless
To continue serving my fate.

18

This Too

Hush! Quiet! We can't speak of this
The walls around us can hear
But we ran away to find bliss
Not return to live in fear

Why can't we celebrate
And see the world around us
Smiles from every country and faith
Are surrounding us

We don't have to be afraid
We can learn from these people
In the land where foundations are laid
A place where we all are equal

So hold my hand
And say with me:
This too, is my land
It has kept me free.

My hands

Stained by choices and regrets
These are my hands
Gripping parts of the world that connect
My memories as I became a man

Holding a beautiful new life
These are my hands
They held my loved ones tight
As their tears ran

Planting seeds in my garden
These are my hands
Calloused for a need to harden
While I watched the seedling stand

Yearning to love once
When I had a plan
This is where I placed my trust
These are my hands.

The Three

One wish
Before departing
Said with great longing

Become a bird!
And get The Three
I want them to be the last ones I see

Out of many
She chose three
And one of them is me.

23

A Different Kind

I used to have all the words
Now I've become speechless
You're different, so I've heard
Maybe it's because I've seen less

Inhale a deep breath
Clear your mind
The day of your death
Shall perceive the different kind.

Survive

Left to fade and decay
My mind reflects
A vast array
Of love to reject

How does this happen?
Search for my answer
A beast to never tap in
An image that rejects laughter

Release the hounds
Uncover the box
I can hear the swift sounds
Of them playing with rocks

You are happy
With simplicity
While gluttony
Erects the evil in thee.

Train

Years ago
I stepped on a train
Chicago snow
It always feels the same

As it went along
Cars, newspapers, skyscrapers
I began to hum the song
The song to meet your maker

I've woken up
To see destruction
I'm broken up
With no direction

Then I found you
Hanging off the train
Can I ask who
Would be this insane?

So I grabbed you
Embraced you
You seemed worth the time
You weren't even mine.

Last Week

Last week
I knew how to smile
I've changed
It might last a while

Last week
I laughed
It's strange
To leave your own raft

Last week
I heard you sing
Now this week
I've ceased to feel anything.

Lovely

There were seven of you
My little lovelies
Chewing on my shoes
When we lived simply

I had to remain
Because you were delicate
I quickly became
Your caring surrogate

You were my own
I loved you all
My little lovelies
You made me enthralled.

Reveal

Peel back the veil
Let me see who you are
At this I cannot fail
A good man traveled far

Sit with me and create
Everything before I go
Do not resuscitate
Don't force fate to flow

Reveal it all
Your innermost vulnerability
Your world will stay small
If it lacks creativity.

What I See

It won't make sense now
It will soon
If you see what I see
You wouldn't hear my tune

My footsteps
The beat to my chapters
A broken book
Urging for something to chase after

I stand before you
To gaze and reflect
Beautifully broken
By a divine architect

I can see his words branded on the world
As I march and stumble
I know that I know nothing
With humility, my world won't crumble

I remove my gaze and close my eyes
Enter the hounds
Only here I cannot lie
I am nowhere to be found

I open my eyes to gaze at the sky
Exeunt the hounds
On that rock I will lie
Far from your sound.

Ultimately

Ultimately
These two must be branded to my name
Forgiving and Understanding is my claim

Ultimately
We were all birthed for each other
To hurt, love, and heal one another

Ultimately
You live for a stranger's smile
It's every small gesture that makes life worthwhile

Ultimately
Your hate will lose your fight
For love saves you in the dark moments of the night.

Printed in the United States
By Bookmasters